Niels Bohr: The Life and Legacy of the Influential Atomic Scientist

By Charles River Editors

About Charles River Editors

Charles River Editors provides superior editing and original writing services across the digital publishing industry, with the expertise to create digital content for publishers across a vast range of subject matter. In addition to providing original digital content for third party publishers, we also republish civilization's greatest literary works, bringing them to new generations of readers via ebooks.

Sign up here to receive updates about free books as we publish them, and visit Our Kindle Author Page to browse today's free promotions and our most recently published Kindle titles.

Introduction

Niels Bohr with Werner Heisenberg at the Copenhagen Conference in 1934

Niels Bohr

"An expert is a person who has made all the mistakes that can be made in a very narrow field."
– Niels Bohr

Sticky, flaky pastries injected with generous dollops of custard or fruit fillings. The iconic, brightly colored building blocks better known as *Lego* bricks. The scenic Nyhavn, a picturesque waterfront and entertainment district featuring a variety of traditional vessels and multicolored houses that color the reflections of the canal's glass-like surface. These are only a few of the plentiful fruits that have blossomed on Danish soil, and they demonstrate some of the many reasons why Denmark has been crowned among the top three happiest countries in the world (out of 155 nations surveyed) for seven consecutive years and counting.

The Danes have incorporated a system that prizes a balance between work and play, the concept of *"hygge,"* solid investments made towards the treatment of mental illness, and a stellar welfare model. That has helped ensure that an endless stream of intellectuals, inventors, creative legends, and pioneers have hailed from Denmark over many centuries, from classical scholar Ada Adler to fabled 16th century astronomer Tycho Brahe. One of the most famous, and important, is Niels Bohr, a world-famous physicist and one of the patriarchs of quantum theory. Given the vibrant, peaceful haven that is Denmark today, it's somewhat ironic that Bohr played an instrumental role in the development of the atomic bomb. Even so, the truth and depth of the matter, much like the self-professed pacifist himself, is far more complex.

Niels Bohr: The Life and Legacy of the Influential Atomic Scientist examines the life and work that made Bohr one of the 20th century's most important scientists. Along with pictures of important people, places, and events, you will learn about Bohr like never before.

Like Father, Like Son

"Every great and deep difficulty bears in itself its own solution. It forces us to change our thinking in order to find it." – Niels Bohr

It was October 7, 1885, the day of Ellen Adler's 25th birthday. Normally, her glossy, dark hair would be pulled back in a neat bun, but today, limp locks framed her face, slick with sweat. As a few servants fanned and fawned over her, dabbing her shiny cheeks with a dry cloth, the midwife between her legs gently coached her to push. Giving birth was as agonizing as it was beautiful, but as soon as the midwife placed the little bundle of joy in her arms, whatever pain she felt promptly melted away. Ellen's mother, Jenny Raphael, thanked her servants and midwife before sending them away, allowing the mother and her newborn some privacy.

Ellen felt a certain sense of nostalgic safety in her mother's estate across Christiansborg Castle in Copenhagen, which is why she requested to have her children there, including her first, Jennifer, two years earlier. She longed for nothing more than to have her father, David Adler, meet his grandson, but the man had died seven years prior. Still, she intended to keep his legacy alive, so she named her first son Niels Henrik David Bohr.

It would be fair to say that the Bohr children – Jenny, Niels, and Harald (born 18 months later in 1887) – were born with silver spoons in their mouths, but the expectations that presumably weighed on the young ones' shoulders could not have been easy to bear. Their father and primary breadwinner of the family, Christian Harald Bohr, carved out a name for himself as an esteemed and popular physiology professor at the University of Copenhagen, and back in 1881, he was rewarded the title of *"Privatdozent."* Christian would later be nominated for a Nobel Prize in 1907, and again the following year for his work concerning the physiology of respiration, but he failed to make the cut both times. Ellen, for her part, was the well-educated daughter of an affluent and exceedingly successful Sephardic Jewish banking magnate and politician.

Christian Bohr

Harald and Niels

The Bohr children may have very well inherited a love for mathematics, science, and logic from their father, but it was Christian's natural and unabating zeal for these subjects, even after hours, that fostered their individual passions. Christian hosted regular dinner parties for colleagues, as well as other scientists and scholars in his fields, and the tightknit group engaged in electrifying discussions and debates as they feasted on various meats, breads, pastries, and wine. Even from a young age, Niels and his siblings were invited to listen in, weigh in, and present questions to the experts themselves.

Niels, an inquisitive child, was often confounded, and thereby all the more intrigued by the scientists' dialogue. He looked forward to these gatherings, and even when he was not permitted to speak, he did not budge from his seat, listening intently for hours on end. The topics mostly revolved around biology and anatomy, concepts that would not appeal to a typical kid at the age of 6, but he was an especially persistent child who practically demanded to know how the world worked. The issue of mechanism vs. vitalism was among the concepts that left the deepest impression on him. Simply put, those who championed mechanism advocated for a methodical, machine-like approach to assessing diseases, biological processes, and so on, whereas the latter preferred a more holistic approach. An excerpt from one of Niels' manuscripts mentioned these meetings: "From my earliest youth, I remember having heard discussions [regarding the ontological nature of living organisms] between Carl Lange, Chievitz, and my father concerning such questions."

The party of intellectuals that young Niels had almost unrestricted access to would be at any scientist's dream dinner party. Johan Chievitz, for one, was a respectable professor of anatomy and the recipient of the Copenhagen Gold Medal in 1879, thanks to a glittering academic résumé. Christian Christiansen, a colleague of Christian Bohr's at the University and founder of the Christiansen Effect, was a physics enthusiast who would later become Niels' instructor. The bespectacled Carl Lange, a professor who specialized in pathological anatomy, made multiple contributions to psychiatry, psychology, and neurology. He is most often associated with the James-Lange Theory of Emotion, which he coined with American psychologist William James.

Christiansen

Lange

When the charismatic and mustachioed Christian wasn't challenging his children with equations or imparting new scientific knowledge, he recounted riveting stories about their ancestors. Christian's father, Henrik, made certain to remind his children of their humble roots and drill into them the value of hard work and perseverance, and Christian was anxious to do the same with his own children. Niels' paternal ancestors were descendants of a German immigrant and soldier named Christian Baar. The 30-year-old Baar first settled in Elsinore (Helsingør) in Eastern Denmark in 1770, but was discharged shortly thereafter. Baar, who would go on to wed four times, was forced to juggle multiple jobs below the pay grade he had grown accustomed to, but he set his ego aside to provide for his growing family. In 1776, the former soldier was registered as a gardener, and 13 years later, he was listed as a janitor at the Øresund Custom House in Helsingør. It was his third marriage with the Norwegian Johanne Engelke Bomholt in 1750 that produced the main heirs who would extend his bloodline, including his two sons, Christian Friedrich Gottfried Bohr and Peter Georg Bohr, Niels' great-grandfather.

It was Baar's sons who sparked the family's affinity with academics and the arts. In 1790, upon Christian Friedrich's departure from Denmark to Norway, he applied for and received a position as a general teacher for local schools. The multi-talented Christian, who was also a musician, was later appointed the organist for a local church in Bergen. It was during this time that he began to expand on his interest in astronomy and mathematics. Not long after the debut of his publications in the forms of both full-length textbooks and articles regarding the aforementioned subjects came the crescendo of his career, when he was inducted in the Royal Academy of Science in 1819, and then the Swedish Academy of Science eight years later. He was such a beloved figure in local circles that the Bishop of Bergen himself penned a memorial about him that ran 48 pages long.

Peter, Niels' grandfather, was the more religious of the pair (most sources claim they subscribed to the Lutheran Christian faith), and he dedicated much of his life to theology. He was first employed as a theology and general teacher at *Den Lærde Skole*, a local grammar school, and later at a grammar school in Nakskov, roughly 130 miles south of Helsingør, before being appointed headmaster of a grammar school in Rønne. Adding to his list of achievements were numerous historical essays, a medley of poems, and a textbook written entirely in Latin.

Along with three of his other brothers, Henrik Georg Christian Bohr (Niels' grandfather) chose to follow in Peter's footsteps. Henrik also pursued theology, and by 1844 he had been appointed headmaster of Copenhagen's Von Westen Institute. Like his father, Henrik was promoted to titular professor in 1860.

Henrik and his wife Caroline produced seven children, six of whom would survive into adulthood and would go on to branch out into various sciences. Henrik, Jr. was a trained engineer and certified attorney who practiced and dominated his field in the Far East. The younger Peter Georg found his calling in philology and was eventually appointed headmaster of the Von Westen Institute. Henrik's three daughters - Augusta, Olivia, and Ida - married a theologian, a vicar, and a mathematics professor, respectively. Then, of course, there was Niels' father, Christian, a two-time Nobel Prize nominee who started his journey with his doctoral thesis on the "pellets of fat suspended in milk."

Niels' maternal ancestors were local celebrities in a different competitive field. Not only do many credit Niels' grandfather, David Adler, with revolutionizing the banking industry, the self-identified National Liberalist served in the city council for two terms and was a well-honored member of Danish Parliament. Moreover, he dabbled in "progressive pedagogy" and "classical philology," and he was revered for his magnanimity and unswerving diligence, despite his immense wealth and status. David, a steadfast subscriber to the Jewish faith, was also applauded for his wholehearted acceptance of other religions, a quality he ingrained in Ellen, who in turn passed it on to her children. Niels' six maternal aunts and uncles also captained impressive careers, venturing into philology, politics, banking, and engineering.

It may have been Christian's insistence upon maintaining a balance between education and recreational activities that made his children so successful. Before his weekend dinner parties, he rounded up the Bohr children and took them on lengthy walks and uphill hikes, taking full advantage of the idyllic Copenhagen scenery. On some Sundays, Niels and his brother Harald boarded a small boat with Christian, and merrily rowed towards the Christianhavn Canals.

Christian, a man of multiple interests, was also something of a sportsman. He funded the football pitches at Tagensvej, a major street located in inner Copenhagen, where he brought his boys whenever he felt the itch to kick a ball around. Such was Christian's ardor for the sport that some biographers claim it was he helped give rise to association football in Denmark. The Bohr brothers took to the sport almost instantly, and they began to practice drills amongst themselves whenever they had the time to spare. During school vacations, they spent much of their time in the Tagensvej football fields, or in the spacious backyard of their grandparents' lavish country house in Nærumgård.

While Niels enjoyed and was quite skilled at filling the post of goalkeeper, his talents were eclipsed by the effortless prowess of his younger brother. Harald, it seemed, had the tallest mountain to scale, but at the same time, he had twice the speed and agility of his siblings. The young man would later earn his bread and butter as a prominent mathematician, and in 1908 he was selected to play for the Danish football team during the year's Summer Olympics. They went on to trounce France 17-1, an Olympic record that earned him the silver medal. Their sister Jennifer went on to make an adequate living as a schoolteacher, another feat in its own right considering the era's restrictions on women.

A picture of the 1908 Olympics team with Harald standing in the back row second from left

Neither Christian nor Ellen had ever expressed much concern about Niels, who was well-behaved, well-mannered, and performed sufficiently enough in his studies. That said, in his earlier years, Niels seemed perfectly content with coasting along in the middle of his class. However, rather than push him, his parents allowed him to develop at his own pace. Indeed, Niels was a late bloomer, but even his parents failed to anticipate the tremendous ripple effect he would one day impose upon the world of science.

Another lesser-explored theme in Niels' life was his fondness of philosophy. Like many of his passions in life, it was one he inherited from his father. Christian was a man of letters both on and off campus, often quoting Faust and Goethe in lectures, conversations, and tongue-lashings alike. The philosopher Harald Høffding, another frequent attendee of Christian's dinner parties, attested to his peer's adoration of philosophy: "Outside the laboratory, he was a keen worshiper of Goethe. When he spoke of practical situations or of views of life, he liked to do so in form of paradoxes and these were as a rule improvised."

Harald Høffding

Niels later summoned memories of Christian passionately reciting Goethe during their excursions and story time by the fireplace. He became rather attached to Goethe himself, and he often borrowed the 18th century polymath's words when he found it difficult to form his own. This is made clear in a letter he later authored to his future wife, in which he included a verse from Goethe's "Wide World & Wide Life":

"Spacious world, capricious life,

Years with honest effort rife.

Tireless searching, firmly founded,

Never ended, often rounded.

Old traditions, well-respected,

Innovations not rejected.

Noble aim, with cheer professed:

Well, we're sure that we've progressed."

   Christian took note of Niels' fascination with philosophy early on, once remarking that his son was "from youth, able to say something about philosophical questions." Niels' attraction to philosophy most likely stemmed from the Bohrs' encouragement of discussion, debate, and exposure to unconventional, but promising ideas. Christian disagreed with some of the opinions held by his colleagues, but he always remained composed and relied on cogent arguments to get his point across. More importantly, he was never disrespectful and leaned away from condescension when handling with the less enlightened, traits that his children absorbed.

Goethe

Niels began his formal education at Gammelholm Latin School in Copenhagen at the age of 7. Prior to the long-awaited Education Act of 1894, Danish schools were vastly underfunded and operated under the Bell-Lancaster method of education, in part due to the devastating and lasting effects of the Napoleonic Wars. The Bell-Lancaster technique, shipped in from industrial England, aimed to cut costs and streamline the system by simplifying the curriculum and unloading the burden on just a handful of instructors. Parents protested and campaigned to broaden and diversify school subjects to no avail, so their children were to make do with the basics of reading, writing, and mathematics. The size of Niels' class, manned by only one instructor, meant that daily lectures were often rushed and restricted by endless rules. Still, Niels was well-disciplined, submitting and completing assignments and exams in a timely manner. He had virtually no problems with his teacher.

Niels' grades gradually improved with time, managing to place between third and fifth in a class of roughly 20 or so pupils. Logic, numbers, and bodies of knowledge and scientific fact came as second nature to the rational youngster, but the delicate art of knitting words together and crafting a storyline, as well as the hunger for learning new terms and phrases so as to better express himself, was another story. His least favorite subject was Danish writing (more specifically, composition), and though he was proficient at reading, spelling, and comprehension, he was often unable or unwilling to follow through with instructions when it came to his writing assignments. When tasked with penning an essay about one of his most memorable trips, he casually submitted a decidedly brief, matter-of-fact piece composed of only two sentences: "A Trip in the Harbor – My brother and I went for a walk in the harbor. There we saw ships land and leave."

Contrary to what one might expect, Niels did not neglect his homework until the last minute. In fact, the pink rectangular block that was his eraser would be whittled down to a nub from all the non-stop scrubbing of failed word connections. He then presented his paper to his instructor proudly the next morning, and he took great offense when the teacher reprimanded him for his laziness. In essence, Niels' scientific mind simply did not understand the need to embellish facts, instead preferring to be concise and to the point. As the story goes, when Niels was later assigned the topic, "Using the Forces of Nature at Home," he was prepared to submit this one-sentence response: "We do not use the forces of nature in our home."

In hindsight, the Latin school's mechanical and largely unchallenging curriculum may have been the reason for young Niels' disinterest in his formal schooling. Outside of the classroom, the boy exhibited an unmatched energy and a zest for learning that were beyond his years. He often posed and sought answers to existential questions, and he eventually developed a habit for taking things apart and studying its different components as a way to help him understand how the world functioned.

The dexterous child soon became the primary handyman of the family, repairing clocks, pocket watches, lamps, and other faulty instruments and devices around the house. Christian took immediate heed of his son's penchant for practical work, and he urged his son to enhance his skills on his own. When the sprocket on the rear of a neighbor's bicycle became fractured, Niels rose to fetch his tools almost at once. Upon his return, he examined the broken sprocket carefully, apparently tinkering with the component so long that it prompted his impatient neighbor to suggest the services of a professional. To this, Christian replied, "Let the boy be. He knows what he is doing."

Apart from Niels' amusing interactions with his writing instructor, there was nothing out of the ordinary about his social life. He was well-liked and had plenty of mates at school, occasionally playing football and other sports with his brawnier friends, but he always considered his brother Harald his best friend. That said, besides their mutual love for football and arithmetic, not much else is known about the sacred relationship between the Bohr brothers.

Bearing this in mind, by assessing the above accounts, one can gather that their shared interests set the foundation for their lifetime bond. Photographs of the Bohr children reveal that the brothers were dressed in matching outfits from an early age, and the pair continued to share a similar style in fashion throughout their life. At the same time, Harald was the yin to Niels' yang. Harald, the more relaxed of the pair, encouraged Niels to venture out of his comfort zone, while the latter kept the former grounded. A mutual friend once noted, "The two are inseparable. I have never known people to be as close as they are."

Christian's conscious avoidance of favoring any of the children helped strengthen the Bohr siblings' bond. He did his best to remain fair and unbiased, cultivating a healthy and wholesome environment free of envy, yet defined by sibling rivalry. To Christian, his children excelled in their own ways – Jennifer was "resilient," Harald was "brilliant," and Niels was "special."

Halfway into Niels' secondary school education – which he continued at Gammelholm –his latent genius started to emerge. The Education Act of 1894 prompted an extensive remodeling of the institution's curriculum and an expansion of its employee roster, which many chroniclers believe ignited Niels' interest in his schooling. Furthermore, the diversification of scientific subjects renewed the young man's passion for that sector, leading him to major in both physics and mathematics during his junior and senior years.

It did not take long for Niels to capture the attention of his physics and mathematics instructors. Initially, they were awed by the student's cognizance of these subjects and often lauded his unflagging enthusiasm. Just a few weeks into the first term, however, they began to grow weary of the student's constant interruptions. Niels was not monkeying around with his seatmates, nor did he aim to stray from the subject at hand in any way. Instead, the teenager was so committed to these subjects that he took the initiative to read up on these fields on his off time. As much as he appreciated the inclusion of these new subjects, he was highly disappointed with the antiquated information in his textbooks. Left without much choice, he began to highlight the erroneous calculations, formulas, dates, and facts in his books, and he jotted down the corrections in the margins.

Naturally, as the teenager's confidence exceeded those of his peers, he had no qualms about speaking out when necessary – even in uncomfortable circumstances – and never hesitated to find fault in his instructors' lectures. The outspoken teenager was so renowned for his "antics" that a few began to direct their questions to him, cutting out the instructor. When one of his classmates inquired about what he would do if he ever stumbled upon a flawed question in one of their exams, without missing a beat, Niels responded, "Why, explain how things really work, of course."

Later on, Niels would credit his father for his interest in physics: "My interest in the study...was awakened while I was still in school, largely owing to the influence of my father." But come 1903, when 17-year-old Niels was awarded his diploma for secondary school, the conflicted teenager was made to confront the first major crossroad moment of his life. Philosophy and physics were placed on the pans of the balance scale, but the weights seesawed dizzyingly in his mind's eye..."

Bohr's Higher Education

"Never express yourself more clearly than you are able to think." – Niels Bohr

Niels was accepted to and duly began his undergraduate studies at the University of Copenhagen. The university, where his father was employed, was by no means a new institution; in fact, it was established roughly four centuries ago and was at this stage, the only proper university in the entire country. Still, space, equipment, and the overall system were minimal, to say the least, housing only five different departments staffed by a measly crew of 48 senior professors. In the same breath, there were many hidden merits in such an arrangement, such as the fact that students had greater access to professors who had been thoroughly vetted.

The conflict within him was ultimately subdued by his decision to select mathematics under Professor Thorvald Thiele and philosophy under Professor Høffding as his majors during freshman year. When Harald joined him at the university two years later, with the younger Bohr enrolling in a few philosophy classes himself, the inseparable duo began to participate in philosophical and scientific discussions conducted by fellow philosophy pupils. And like Harald, Niels resumed his active lifestyle, ensuring that he allotted himself quick breaks between his assignments and projects, as well as study time prior to tests and examinations. He jogged around campus, took hikes along the many trails scattered throughout the city, and participated in casual football matches. Even so, his mind was undoubtedly fixated – or some might even say, preoccupied – with an unending number of equations and scientific theories.

A former teammate later reminisced about a comical incident that transpired during a match against some German players. Niels, a more than competent goalkeeper, initially stopped almost every ball that came hurtling his way, but the German players were equally seasoned, which resulted in a tie. Through a series of practiced manipulations, Niels' teammates succeeded in moving the ball to their opponents' half of the pitch, only for one of their rivals to sweep in and steal the ball at the last minute. The spectators leapt up to their feet in near unison, but their looks of astonishment soon morphed to ones of pure incredulity, for Niels had somehow zoned out amidst the chaos and was working out a mathematical equation against the goalpost. It took the piercing shrieks of several spectators (and presumably the lightning-fast blur in his peripheral vision) for Niels to pay attention to the game again.

Notwithstanding his evident obsession with science and numbers, it seemed for some time that Niels would choose a philosophical path. To start with, he passed the *Filosofikum* with flying colors, a compulsory end-of-the-year examination for all philosophy students. He had a genuine appreciation for the subject rarely seen in teenagers his age, not to mention an understanding and an ability to venture outside of the box to form unorthodox, but sound solutions.

All philosophy courses, taught between a trinity of philosophy teachers, revolved around three principal textbooks, all authored by Høffding, the faculty head: *Outlines of Psychology, History of Modern Philosophy,* and *Formula Logic for Use at Lectures,* a direct translation of *Formel Logik til Brug ved Forelæsninger.* Between the 1st of September and the 1st of June, all pupils of philosophy were expected to complete a minimum of four hours of lectures each week, each term concluding with a formal oral examination.

As university students are wont to do, many of Niels' classmates groused about the workload and often raced against the clock to complete their projects. Niels, on the other hand, was one of Høffding's star pupils. He had known the philosophy pundit for years, so he was more accustomed to his diction and choice of words, making it easy for the young man to draw level with his teaching style. Still, although Niels would later admit that he was not the first to do so, he identified problems in Høffding's textbooks – particularly *Formula Logic for Use at Lectures* – with certitude, and he unabashedly made his voice heard. David Favrholdt, author of *Niels Bohr's Philosophical Background,* described one of these corrections: "In the edition from 1903 [of *Formula Logic*], Høffding exemplifies the principle of duality (the principle of the excluded middle) and writes that a 'concept (B) must either contain another concept (A) or its negation (a).' Here, 'either-or' is used in the exclusive sense. Obviously, Bohr had pointed out to Høffding that this is nonsense: a concept can in fact include both another concept and its negation."

Høffding was, as one might expect, anything but pleased by Niels' admittedly smart aleck behavior, but he eventually seemed to accept the teenager's criticisms, and occasionally he even sought out the prodigy's advice. Proof of Høffding's faith in the young man can be found in the numerous letters exchanged between them regarding the matter. One such letter reads:

"Dear Student Bohr,

I hereby send you the first page of the new edition of *Formel Logik*, asking you to look it through in your usual critical way. Please write your remarks, if any, on a piece of paper and enclose it – I do hope that I am not causing you too much trouble by asking you to do this.

Yours Sincerely,

Harald Høffding."

Despite everything on his plate, during his sophomore and junior years at university, Niels managed to squeeze physics classes into his already hectic schedule, thereby allowing himself to play the field before settling upon a career choice. His instructor for general physics was Christian Christiansen, and an anecdote recalls a humorous exchange between Niels and his physics professor.

One morning, Professor Christiansen attempted to flummox his students by posing this challenge: "How does one determine the height of a skyscraper using only a barometer (an instrument that calculates atmospheric pressure)?" After some consideration, Niels scribbled his answer on a sheet of paper: "Easy – first, you tie a long length of rope around the barometer. Then, you lower it from the skyscraper's rooftop. The length of the string, plus the length of the barometer will give you the precise height of the building."

Professor Christiansen, who at this point had suffered through enough of Niels' unintentionally condescending responses, was understandably livid. He quickly dismissed his answer and slapped "FAIL" onto his paper, but an embittered Niels demanded justice. He was supposedly so insistent that Christiansen grudgingly agreed to summon a neutral party to settle the argument. Come judgment day, the negotiator concluded that while Niels' response was technically correct, he did not use, nor did he elaborate on, standard concepts in physics. The arbiter felt it unjust to fail him, but at the same time, he was apprehensive about disregarding what was in actuality, a logical answer.

To remedy this quandary, both the arbiter and professor agreed to allow Niels to present them with a new, physics-related response in the form of an oral presentation that lasted no more than six minutes. Much to their initial dismay, the student spent an entire five minutes with a puckered forehead, lost in thought. When the professor anxiously warned him about what little time was left on the clock, Niels spoke up for the first time. He had come up with various answers, he replied, but was unsure about which the professor preferred. He then proceeded to rattle them off one at a time without taking a breath: "First of all, you could take a barometer up to the rooftop, release it over the edge, and measure the amount of time it takes to reach the ground, but doing so would result in a broken barometer. If you did this in the morning, you could gauge the height of the barometer, place it in position, measure the length of the instrument's shadow before juxtaposing the measurements with the length of the skyscraper's shadow, and deduce the height of the skyscraper from there on out."

Unaware, or perhaps indifferent to the professor's stuttering objections, Niels continued, "If you are looking for a more 'scientific' method, I suggest you snip off a piece of rope, tie it around your barometer, and swing it like a pendulum from one end to the other – first, on the first floor, and then again on the rooftop. Unfortunately, you were not at all specific about the skyscraper's amenities, so the possibilities do not end there. If the skyscraper is outfitted with emergency staircases, one could then trot up the stairs, create notches on every floor of the building, and later, add them all together."

Finally, he provided the simple response that Professor Christiansen was so desperately searching for: "Now, if an unimaginative response is what you so seek, I suppose you could also use the barometer to measure the air pressure on both the ground floor and the rooftop of the skyscraper, then convert the difference into a height of air."

The professor heaved a sigh of relief, but Niels, to his great exasperation, was not quite finished: "All that said, since you are always urging us to explore ideas on less charted planes, I feel as if I have the perfect answer. Why not knock on the custodian's door and offer him a gleaming new barometer in exchange for the ever-elusive dimensions of the skyscraper?"

As funny as that exchange is, most scholars believe that it never happened, instead, reducing the tale to an apocryphal story. Many argue that it is highly unlikely that Niels would have gambled his potential future for what was such an obvious question. Moreover, it was not in his nature to be so determinedly difficult and verbose for the sake of some cheap laughs.

In addition to general physics, the University's Faculty of Physics also provided courses in astronomy and inorganic chemistry, both of which Niels enrolled in. Niels was eager to roll up his sleeves and conduct the experiments required for the latter subject, but it appeared that his motor skills occasionally failed to keep up with his overactive brain. He fared well in his assignments and tests, both written and oral, but he was so clumsy that he unwittingly broke the record for most beakers, tubes, and other lab equipment shattered in a term. This fazed him at first, given how handy he was outside of the laboratory, but he kept at it.

Ultimately, the clumsy student's devotion to completing his practical projects did little to help him succeed. Legend has it that when Niels was conducting one of his experiments at the laboratory of the Polytechnic Institute, where all the research and laboratory work were conducted, the helplessly uncoordinated student set off one of his many explosions. Niels Bjerrum, a teaching assistant who was pursuing his Master's degree at the time, was seated behind a desk just outside of the laboratory. On top of the deafening boom, the lamps overhead began to swing, as did the ground beneath him, but he did not so much as flinch. Instead, he continued on with his work as the concerned students around him shuffled over to investigate. Without ever looking up from the journals and textbooks laid out in front of him, he waved them away. "It's only Bohr," he grumbled with a shake of his head.

By this point, Niels had spent the first half of his undergraduate career trying different fields of science, but finally, in February 1905, the 20-year-old was presented with a pivotal opportunity that would cement the undeniable truth lingering in the back of his mind. That month, the Royal Danish Academy of Sciences announced that a gold medal would be gifted to anyone who could delineate and accurately measure the surface tensions of liquids via the surface vibrations of liquid jets, a theory first proposed by Lord Rayleigh back in 1879. The majority of those vying for the gold were legitimate veterans in the field who were pursuing their doctorates, teachers of the subject, or professionals backed by government grants. Nevertheless, Niels, though still two years away from securing his bachelor's diploma, was resolved to bring home the gold.

Lord Rayleigh

Bohr as a young adult

Contestants were expected to fashion the precision instruments required to test the theory in question on their own, which meant that hours upon hours of toiling away in the laboratory lay in store for him, but Niels was never one to shy away from a challenge and remained undeterred, in spite of his less than appealing track record in experimentation.

The willing assistance of his supportive father was once again key in the success of what was to be Niels' greatest endeavor yet. Christian knew that his son was most productive when working in solitude, and he realized the school lacked the proper facilities and personal space, so he offered his personal physiology lab to Niels. Here, Niels worked almost every day for several months in a row, opting to work in the still of the night to avoid the distractions of traffic and other jarring noises.

Thankfully, Christian routinely checked up on his son, and when he saw how engrossed his son was in his experimentation, Niels was sternly ordered to halt with his self-destructive behavior at once. Eventually, it reached the point that Christian urged him to put pen to paper. The younger Bohr did as he was told and retired to his maternal grandmother's country home just a few doors away from Christiansborg Castle to compose his written research. This was just as well, for on October 30, 1906, owing to Niels' dogged focus and Christian's prudent guidance, the 21-year-old submitted a brilliant paper that earned him the coveted gold medal on February 23, 1907. The stellar student, in the Academy's words, had done so by "[including] in his work essential improvements on Rayleigh's theory by taking into account the influence of the liquid's viscosity and of the ambient air, and by extending the earlier theory from infinitesimal to arbitrarily large amplitudes."

Niels' paper, written in Danish, sailed under the radar until 1908, when he presented an English version of his research to the Royal Society of London. The original, unedited version of Niels' prize paper has since vanished into the vortex of time, but a copy replicated by his younger brother, Harald, can be found in the Bohr Archives. The paper was published by the Royal Society in 1909. Not only was this Niels' first official publication, it was the product of the only primarily experimental work he had ever conducted throughout the course of his illustrious career. All research that followed was restricted to theoretical physics.

Niels was made to share the commendation with Peder Oluf Pederson, a future professor of electrical engineering and major contributor to electrotechnology who was older than him by a little over a decade. As Pederson's age suggests, such an achievement was nearly unprecedented, especially for a mere undergraduate who had yet to receive his diploma.

The handsome gilded medallion represented far more than just a well-deserved victory, because it marked the point that Bohr realized he was destined for the world of physics. Shortly after the triumph, Niels' philosophy professor wrote him the following letter of felicitation for his prize paper, entitled "Determination of Surface Tension of Water by the Method of Jet Vibration." The letter read:

"Dear Niels Bohr,

It was a great pleasure for me to learn this evening at the Academy that your paper was rewarded with a prize. I congratulate you on this fine distinction that you have won at such an early age, and I take this opportunity to thank you for your valuable collaboration.

Sincerely yours,

Harald Høffding."

In 1907, Niels received his bachelor's diploma, plump with distinctions. He was still just 22.

1909 would prove to be one of the most memorable years of Bohr's life. Harald would cast a shadow over his older brother once again, earning his master's degree in April of that year, but Niels, who only received his for his thesis (an introduction to the electron theory of metals) 8 months later, took it in stride. Some now believe it was his transformative summer that helped soften the blow.

In part to celebrate Harald's most recent achievement, the Bohr brothers took about a week off and invited a small group of friends on a short trip around the Danish countryside. Upon their return, they stopped by the home of Niels Erik Nørlund, a classmate of Harald's. It was there that Niels met Nørlund's 19-year-old sister, Margrethe. Niels was instantly taken with the bubbly beauty, mesmerized by her distinctive laugh and the way her hair danced when she spoke. Her soothing voice and the tenderness of her gentle ways, which reminded Niels of his mother's kindness, drew him even closer.

Niels and Margrethe

In just a matter of months, she had his heart, and the feeling was mutual. Margrethe was struck by the 24-year-old's wisdom and maturity, and she found herself clinging onto his every word. What set the smartly-dressed, bushy-browed gentleman apart from the rest, she later confided in a friend, was his "modesty" and "friendliness," and above all, "those lovely eyes" of his.

Even more endearing to Niels was the fact that Margrethe did not require the constant attention that most girls her age sought after. She understood how important Niels' work was to him and rarely complained about a delay in his letters. Her consideration was as needed as it was appreciated, for he would dive into his doctoral research just weeks after he received his Master's degree.

Meanwhile, Niels' relationship with Harald only continued to strengthen. Rather than allow the natural feelings of sibling rivalry to poison their rapport, the Bohr brothers – who were working on their doctoral theses simultaneously – continued to work alongside and assist one another. Harald was to Niels the ideal study partner, for his brother's expertise in mathematics often hauled him out of ruts, and vice versa. The pair often dictated their papers to the other and listened attentively to both advice and constructive criticism.

For Niels' doctoral thesis, he chose to further his shallow work on the electron theory of metals. It was during this period of research that he first happened upon Max Planck's quantum theory of radiation, which characterized energy as small parcels or packets known as "quanta." This was also his first discovery of what is now known as the "Bohr-van Leeuwen Theorem," as defined by Kiel University: "The state of a classical many-particle system cannot be altered by turning on a magnetic field: in particular, a liquid will remain a liquid and a crystal will remain a crystal."

Planck

In early 1911, Niels conducted his defense for his doctoral dissertation, which he called *"Studier over metallernes elektrontheori,"* or in English, "Studies on the Electron Theory of Metals." J. R. Nielsen, the editor of *Early Work (1905-1911),* explained the content of Niels' dissertation in the following passage, as well as the latent issues that would inspire his upcoming work: "[The paper was] a purely theoretical work that again exhibited a sovereign mastery of the vast subject he had chosen...This theory, which pictures the metallic state as a gas of electrons moving more or less freely in the potential created by the positively charged atoms disposed in a regular lattice, accounted qualitatively for the most varied properties of metals; but it ran into many difficulties as soon as a quantitative treatment was attempted on the basis of then accepted principles of classical electrodynamics." Niels himself concluded, "It does not seem possible at the present stage of the development of the electron theory to explain the magnetic properties of bodies from this theory."

Eventually, he formulated a list of methods that highlighted the problem areas of certain principles from existing theories, most notably that it was impossible to accurately identify the magnetic properties of metals via any classical theories. At this stage, Niels was aware of the importance of his newfound conclusion, but not even the physicist in-the-making himself could estimate the true magnitude of his discovery. As Nielsen put it, "The rigor of his analysis gave him...the firm conviction of the necessity of a radical departure from classical electrodynamics for the description of atomic phenomena." In other words, he was one crucial step closer to the atomic model, which many consider to be the magnum opus of his scientific career.

Niels was granted his doctoral degree in May that same year and dedicated his dissertation to Christian, who died after a heart attack just three months earlier. Again, his work would not be properly acknowledged until Hendrika Johanna van Leeuwen, a Dutch physicist, chanced upon it eight years later.

For the first few weeks of the summer that followed, Niels briefly hung up his lab coat to spend some quality time with Harald and Margrethe. The love birds hopped aboard boats and cruises, sailing across the shimmering waters of the Baltic Sea, ambled through the countryside, and spent many an evening drinking and laughing in Tivoli. The courtship came to an end not long thereafter, for Niels planned to journey abroad to further his studies. Before he left, he delicately requested Margrethe's hand in marriage, a modest, but felicitous proposal that she happily accepted.

Career Highlights

"Anyone who is not dizzy after his first acquaintance with quantum of action, has not understood a word." – attributed to Niels Bohr

Back in 1897, English physicist and future Nobel laureate Sir Joseph John Thomson divulged to the world his pioneering discovery of "corpuscles" (later rechristened "electrons") in cathode rays. Niels was one of countless scientists around the world who were immediately intrigued by the finding, which ignited an explosion of research in the field. The atom, previously regarded as a solid sphere, was a one-dimensional entity no more; rather, scientists began to focus on the relationships between the complementary subatomic particles found in all atoms. This was especially true of electrons, which carried a charge of negative electricity, and protons, which were equipped with a positive charge.

Thomson

Niels, like many in his field, was itching to work with Sir Thomson at Cambridge, where he governed the Cavendish laboratory. Shortly after receiving his doctoral degree in 1911, he was granted this momentous opportunity. Thus, in the fall of that year, he arrived in Cambridge, a trip sponsored by his alma mater.

Niels wasted no time traveling to the Cavendish laboratory, where he introduced himself to Sir Thomson for the first time. To the slight disappointment of the burgeoning theoretical physicist, the interaction between them was somewhat strained by a language barrier and incompatible ideas, as well as Niels' somewhat assertive style as a student. Just a few minutes into their first conversation, Niels blithely made note of the mistakes in Thomson's work with excruciating detail. He later confessed that he had done so in an ingenuous attempt to gain his new mentor's respect. It is unclear whether this ultimately factored into the dissolution of their collaboration, but it most likely bruised Thomson's ego in some way. Even so, Thomson agreed to part with some advice.

Frustratingly, Niels came upon one dead end after another when it came to his research and experimental work. Although Thomson had never spelled it out in actual words, Niels was under the impression that the aging physicist's passion for the field was slowly, but surely fading. Adding to Niels' annoyance was the fact that Thomson seemed to be putting off the younger physicist's paper and research, depriving him of the analysis and feedback he had been promised.

"[To Niels,] Thomson was a genius who showed the way to everybody," John Heilbron of Oxford University later explained. "But when he got there, he found out that Thomson was busy showing the way to other people, and also following his own research."

Bohr's professional relationships with his other peers at Cambridge were not much better, as illustrated in his letters to Margrethe during this time. James Jeans, a mathematician, was friendly and approachable enough, but he was described as much too meek to challenge Bohr's ideas and engage in the stimulating debate he so desired. The Irish physicist Joseph Larmor, based in Cambridge at the time, appeared to be something of a snob; he refused to even acknowledge Niels' work since it was not written in English and had not been published in any reputable English journal.

As the weeks dragged on, Niels became increasingly aggravated by the lack of progress with his research under Thomson. It pained him to admit it, but the partnership was not a good fit. Some chroniclers now believe that the older physicist may have harbored some resentment for his brief protege in his later years, likely because Niels was among the first to disprove his "plum pudding" model. Thomson's concepts were then branded as archaic and "worthless." As Ernest Rutherford indelicately put it, they were "for a museum of scientific curiosities."

Niels' failure to properly collaborate with Thomson was to him a source of deep mortification, but it certainly would not dissuade him from uncovering the truths of physics. If anything, it renewed his motivation to study the perplexing, yet gripping field. Before the end of his collaboration with Thomson, Bohr was granted the privilege of attending one of Ernest Rutherford's lectures. The New Zealand-born physicist, who also held the title of 1st Baron Rutherford of Nelson, first shot to international fame with his discovery of the element radon, as well as the notion of radioactive half-life and his coining of the terms "alpha" and "beta radiation." Just three years prior, Rutherford was presented with the Nobel Prize in Chemistry "for his investigations into the disintegration of the elements, and the chemistry of radioactive substances."

Rutherford

By the time of his lecture, Rutherford had made new waves with his discovery of the atom's nucleus. Niels learned of Rutherford's most recent and ongoing project, which focused discharging alpha articles at various targets and from differing heights to better understand the atom.

Rutherford's trials with gold foil were most compelling to Niels. The majority of the particles succeeded in penetrating the foil, but on some occasions, a particle ricocheted off the glossy sheet. An astounded Rutherford likened the atom to a minuscule solar system, a complicated entity surrounded by floating, or "orbiting" electrons. The alpha particles' effortless penetration of the sheet, Rutherford concluded, was due to the wide space between the nucleus and the electrons. Those that "bounced back," he theorized, must have made contact with the "mass-possessing nucleus." This knowledge, which confirmed that the bulk of the atom's mass was housed within its nucleus, became the foundation of his budding theory.

Niels took a liking to Rutherford at once, so much so that he chose to relocate to Manchester after his stint with Thomson. Rutherford was chiefly involved in experimental physics, whereas Niels considered himself a theoretician of the subject, but the laureate spotted the brilliance and drive within the young man and agreed to take him on as a student.

Fortunately, the pair got along famously, and despite their differences in opinions, they remained lifelong comrades. Rutherford's peers quickly noticed the unlikely alliance that developed between them. Rutherford, then known for his less-than-savory opinions on theoretical physics, was often asked about Bohr and what it was that set him apart from the rest. To this, Rutherford dryly replied, "He's a football player!"

As close as they were, their different backgrounds posed its fair share of problems. Some now believe that Rutherford's disinclination for theoretical physics prevented Niels from fully spreading his wings. With the experimental proof provided by Rutherford, Niels began to explore the concept of isotopes (atoms of elements with different atomic mass but identical atomic numbers). He also conducted further research on the process of radioactive displacement, which describes the conversion of one element to another when the atomic number of the first element is altered. Niels presented this theory to Rutherford with much excitement, only to have his bubble burst by his mentor, who demanded proper evidence before he would even consider such a bold concept.

As it turned out, Bohr was right. In the years that followed, other scientists who conducted similar, but independent research released evidence that supported his original theory. Thankfully, Niels never demonstrated any hard feelings. Not only did he gracefully step aside, allowing the later scientists to claim credit of the discovery unopposed, he was tactful enough to refrain from rubbing it in Rutherford's face.

At this point in his life, it appeared that Niels had come to terms with the nonconformity of his ideas and the potential backlash they attracted. He carried on with his research based on Rutherford's model of the atom, resolved to developing his own "quantum" explanation of the atom and its workings.

One of the most prominent hurdles he faced was the problematic nature of Rutherford's model. Rutherford, whose perception of physics was largely shaped by Newtonian laws, asserted that electrons in orbit gradually lost energy due to the emission of radiation before "collapsing" back into the nucleus. Before Rutherford, both Planck and Einstein had already caused a disruption in the physics world by contradicting certain laws of classical physics in terms of light and radiation.

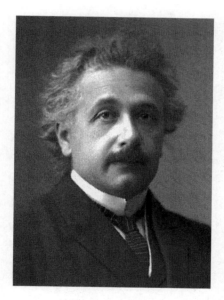

Einstein

A picture of Bohr with James Franck, Einstein and Isidor Isaac Rabi

Niels, who detected an invisible bridge that connected Rutherford's theory to those of Planck and Einstein, was about to cause an even bigger commotion. He dove into this new chapter of his research in the spring of 1912, and his addiction to this work was reinvigorated, for he was now certain that he could plug the holes of Rutherford's model with the help of Planck's Constant. He scratched notes into his journals, crossed out and redid eye-watering equations, and tossed crumpled balls of paper away throughout the night, determined to complete his work before the day of his wedding. His goal was to formulate an equation that would prove that "atoms could only exist in discrete states," each marked by its own value in energy. This same concept would later allow him to describe the brackets of lines seen in the light radiated by hydrogen atoms.

Niels later wrote about this key period of research, "In the spring of 1912, I became convinced that the electronic constitution of the Rutherford atom was governed throughout by the quantum of action."

After about four months in Manchester, Niels returned to Copenhagen just in time for the big day. On August 1, 1912, Niels and Margrethe exchanged their vows in a two-minute civil ceremony before the chief of police and a small, exclusive group of family and friends. Harald served as his best man. The actual wedding itself was rather hastily executed, but the extravagant festivities, organized by Niels' new mother-in-law, certainly were not, and as one might have predicted, the socially bashful groom was not pleased. When the disgruntled groom learned about the fanfare, he reportedly grumbled, "How is it really possible to take three hours for a dinner? Can't we take a ferry at 19:00?"

The couple opted not to have a traditional religious ceremony from the very beginning of their engagement, but Niels only tendered his resignation to the Lutheran Church three months before the wedding. The philosopher at heart had been transfixed with the notion of religion for some time as a child, but at the age of 27, upon severing all ties, he revealed that he was "no longer taken by it." His wife echoed his sentiments: "For me, it was exactly the same. [Interest in religion] disappeared completely."

Niels and Margrethe went on to have six sons, named Christian, Harald, Hans Henrik, Erik, Aage, and Ernest. Four of their children lived to adulthood, as Christian, their oldest son, was tragically killed in a boating accident at the age of 19, and Harald died due to complications from meningitis. Naturally, the untimely deaths of Bohr's young sons left a hole in his heart that would remained unfilled for the rest of his life, but through all the ups and downs of his career and personal life, Margrethe remained an unwaveringly loyal, trustworthy, and fulfilling companion. She provided Niels with animated conversation, and her adventurous personality paired well with his. The couple's fondness for one another is best captured in one black-and-white photograph, which was taken a few years into their marriage. In the photograph, the couple is seen riding their motorcycle on a dirt road. Margrethe, whose arms are locked around Niels' waist, is grinning from ear to ear; Niels, on the other hand, is leaning forward, his forehead lined with concentration.

In addition to being a loving mother and affectionate spouse, Margrethe was an ally who was not afraid to talk sense into her husband when needed. Niels referred to her as "my little one...locked away as [my] heart's treasure." Richard Courant, a close friend, said of them, "Some people have speculated about the lucky circumstances which combined to make Niels so successful. I think the ingredients of his life were by no means matter of chance, but deeply ingrained in the structure of his personality...It was not luck, rather, deep insight, which led him to find in young years his wife, who… had such a decisive role in making his whole scientific and personal activity possible and harmonious."

Days after the wedding, Niels and Margrethe embarked on a semi-continental honeymoon, first vacationing in Norway before traveling to England. It was during their visit to Manchester that Margrethe made the acquaintance of Ernest and Mary Rutherford for the first time. Much to Niels' delight, Margrethe adored them, so much so that the quartet began to spend plenty of time together on the weekends.

Following a last hurrah in Scotland, the couple returned to Copenhagen, where Niels resumed his research on the absorption of alpha particles at the University. Perhaps feeling somewhat guilty about having missed work for some time, the young physicist kicked into high gear. One of his colleagues, Jens Rud Nielsen, remembered that Bohr "would come into the yard, pushing his bicycle faster than anybody else. He was an incessant worker, and seemed always to be in a hurry..."

In the months of July, September, and November of 1913, three of Niels' papers were published in the *Philosophical Magazine,* an English scientific journal. The series, now collectively referred to as "On the Constitution of Atoms and Molecules: Parts I, II, & III," was nicknamed "The Trilogy." Apart from detailing the foundations of his soon-to-be finalized theory, Niels proved that the chemical properties of elements were directly influenced by valence electrons, which occupied the "highest stable orbit." More significantly, he had essentially provided the reasoning behind the nature of the periodic table, which, in effect, spawned a new scientific discipline now known as "quantum chemistry."

In the early months of 1913, Niels' colleague H. M. Hansen anxiously presented to him the formula of Johann Jakob Balmer in experimental spectroscopy, one that aimed to describe the "spectrum" of the hydrogen atom. Niels was overjoyed to have finally found research that aligned with his. He said, "As soon as I saw Balmer's formula, it was immediately clear to me."

Shortly afterwards, he placed the final touches on what is now the "Bohr Model." The Chemistry Department of the University of Purdue breaks down the basic rules of Niels' model:

"1. The electron in a hydrogen atom travels around the nucleus in a circular orbit.

2. The energy of the electron in an orbit is proportional to its distance from the nucleus. The further the electron is from the nucleus, the more energy it has.

3. Only a limited number of orbits with certain energies are allowed. In other words, the orbits are quantized.

4. The only orbits that are allowed are those for which the angular momentum of the electron is an integral multiple of Planck's constant divided by 2.

5. Light is absorbed when an electron jumps to a higher energy orbit, and emitted when an electron falls into a lower energy orbit.

6. The energy of the light emitted or absorbed is exactly equal to the difference between the energies of the orbits."

Shaun C. Ramsey, author of "Niels Bohr: Odyssey of the Atom," explained, "Niels...stated for the hydrogen atom, the potential energy of an electron in the nth energy level is equal to the negative value of the Rydberg constant, multiplied by Planck's constant and the speed of light, divided by the square of the principal quantum number: $E_n = -(Rhc)/n^2$. This equation follows

Coulomb's law, which states that the energy of attraction between subjects that are oppositely charged must have a negative value...those opposite bodies are negative electron and a positive electron."

Thanks to this work, scientists now realized that changes in atoms – in the eyes of quantum theory – were not quick, one-step conversions, but rather intricate processes with multiple steps. It is important to note that Bohr's admittedly primitive theory applied only to atoms with one electron, but the discovery inspired a wave of new and relevant research, a feat that was not lost on him: "The whole field of work has indeed from a very lonely state suddenly got into a desperately crowded one where almost everybody seems hard at work."

By 1914, Bohr had been granted a teaching position in physics at the University of Copenhagen. He was then employed at Manchester's Victoria University, where he retained a similar title, for the next two years.

The demand for Niels, now 31, continued to heighten. Following the end of his contract at the institution in Manchester, he was rehired, this time as a professor of theoretical physics, at the University of Copenhagen. During this time, he began to campaign and raise funds for a proper institute that would be devoted to this specific field. He appealed to the school's board, as well as the Danish Parliament, pursuing the matter relentlessly until it received approval in 1918. About three years later, the Copenhagen Institute for Theoretical Physics was open for business, and Niels served as the institute's director. Later on, he appealed again to the university board on behalf of Harald, suggesting a separate institute for mathematics. The request was granted roughly two decades later, and Harald served as the mathematical institute's first director.

In 1922, Niels reached another major milestone when he was gifted the Nobel Prize on atomic theory, "for his services in the investigation of the structure of atoms and of the radiation emanating from them." Apart from the usual acknowledgments that typically came with such speeches, he gleefully proclaimed to the riveted spectators that "missing element number 72" had been identified. The laureate gave the element its name – Hafnium, the Latin name for "Copenhagen" – some years later.

With the plump sum he was awarded as a complement to the Nobel Prize, Bohr purchased a country home in Tisvilde. The manor, where the couple frequently summered, was dubbed "Lynghuset," and it was a charming home with a thatched roof built atop a low dune and tucked away in the fringes of the Tisdvilde Forest. Niels and Margrethe were especially fond of Lynghuset, which provided their sons with swathes of natural terrain to explore.

Lynghuset's scenic surroundings also provided Bohr with the silence and tranquility he needed for his research. He erected a smaller, similarly thatched house just a few feet away from his summer home solely for this purpose. His office, known as "The Pavilion," doubled as a place of conference for him and his colleagues. Not unlike his familial relationship with Christian's former peers, Niels' colleagues became "uncles" to his sons.

With the Nobel Prize tucked under his belt, it did not take long for Bohr to garner the attention of his idols. None other than Einstein himself is said to have been one of his greatest admirers. The pair met in person for the first time in April 1920, when Niels, then 35, was invited to Berlin. The pair instantly clicked, as evidenced by the letters they exchanged after their initial meeting. Einstein wrote to him, "Not often in life has a person, by his mere presence, given me such joy as you did... I have the pleasure of seeing your youthful face before me, smiling and explaining. I have learned much from you, especially also about your attitude regarding scientific matters." Bohr responded, "To me it was one of the greatest experiences ever to meet you and talk with you, and I cannot express how grateful I am for all the friendliness with which you met me on my visit to Berlin."

Despite the warm feelings, there was no shortage of clashing opinions between the two, which was yet another testament to the strength of their friendship. During the 1927 Solvay Conference, Einstein attempted to unravel Heisenberg's "position-momentum uncertainty principle" with theoretical physics. Three years later, he launched a similar attack upon the time-energy uncertainty principle, a derivative of Heisenberg's work. Both times, Bohr countered Einstein's arguments with theories and supporting calculations that supported Heisenberg's principles. Then, in 1935, Einstein – this time backed by Nathan Rosen and Boris Podolsky – attempted to find fault with the inconsistency of quantum mechanics, and again, Bohr contradicted him. Bohr would later document their debates in a book he entitled *Albert Einstein – Philosopher Scientist*.

A picture of Einstein (front row, middle) and Bohr (second row, far right) at the 1927 Solvay Conference

Abraham Pais, a mutual friend of both men, made the following remark about them: "Both would speak with intense enthusiasm and optimism about work they were engaged in, and had enormous powers of concentration...Their prime concern was always with what they did not understand, rather than with past achievements...They differed in their views regarding the interpretation of quantum mechanics. They argued frequently about it, particularly over the concept of 'complementarity'...By and large, however, similarity outweighed disparity. Both had a deep need for simplicity, in thought and in behavior...They took science very seriously, but to them it was ultimately a game...The greatest similarity, though, was that Einstein and Bohr were both scientists without whom the birth of that uniquely 20th-century mode of thought, quantum physics, is unthinkable."

Meanwhile, Bohr's list of accolades continued to grow. In 1923, he was inducted as a foreign member of the Royal Netherlands Academy of Arts and Sciences, and three years later, he was granted membership in the Royal Society of London. In addition to the Nobel Prize, his collection of commendations included the Hughes Medal (1921), the Matteucci Medal (1923), the Franklin Medal (1926), the Copley Medal (1938), the Order of the Elephant (1947), and the Sonning Prize (1961). Furthermore, he was recognized as an *honoris causa*, or honorary doctor, of the following universities and institutions: Copenhagen, Cambridge, London, Birmingham, Manchester, Oxford, Liverpool, Kiel, Edinburgh, California, Providence, and Oslo (1923-1939); Princeton, McGill, Glasgow, Sorbonne, Aberdeen, Lund, New York, Athens, Aarhus, Basel, Macalester, Roosevek, Minnesota, Bombay, Calcutta, Warsaw, Harvard, Cambridge (Massachusetts), Rockefeller, and Zagreb (1945-1962).

In 1932, Carlsberg Group, a Danish brewery, chose to honor Bohr's achievements. The iconic brewery, which dedicated some of its laboratory space to the research of natural sciences, gifted the theoretical physicist with an "honorary residence" next door to its facilities in Valby, just outside of Copenhagen. Jacob Christian Jacobsen, the founder of the brewery, once occupied the residence, and before his death, he insisted that it be inhabited by "a man or woman deserving of esteem from the community by reason of services to science, literature, art, or for other reasons." The Bohr family moved into this new home – outfitted with a bottomless tap hooked up to the brewery – in Valby later that year, and they lived there for free for the next three decades.

Bohr's Final Years

"How wonderful that we have met with a paradox. Now we have some hope of making progress." – attributed to Niels Bohr

Bohr was not one to involve himself in the thorny entanglements of politics, but towards the start of the 1930s, all this changed. He was among the few who took the gradual, but momentous rise of the Nazis seriously. He scrutinized their rambling texts and analyzed their poisonous propaganda, sounding the alarm whenever he was afforded the opportunity, but the rest of his peers did little more than laugh nervously and sweep all concerns under the rug.

Just as Bohr feared, when Hitler gained dictatorial powers in 1933, the Nazi leader promptly began persecuting Jews, starting by stripping all Jews of their posts. Bohr was among the first to extend aid to Jewish scientists based in Germany, offering arrangements for accommodations, available positions, and a slew of other resources in Copenhagen. He was especially worried about the safety of Otto Frisch, the nephew of his colleague, Lise Meitner. Frisch later revealed how deeply grateful he was for Bohr's selfless actions, comparing the physicist to a benevolent fatherly figure who exuded warmth and hospitality. His interference, wrote Frisch in a letter to his mother, was "an act of the good Lord."

Meitner

Frisch

Undaunted by the Nazis, Niels continued his dangerous tour around Germany and its surrounding nations in 1934. He hoped to coax as many Jewish scientists as he could out of Germany, promising them homes in Copenhagen, as well as lab space, funding, and the safety of their families. Along with his brother Harald and a handful of other Danish scholars, Bohr proceeded to establish the Danish Committee for the Support of Refugee Intellectuals. That same year, his burden was exacerbated by the death of his eldest son, but Bohr would not allow himself to shirk what he felt were his responsibilities, thus forcing himself to forge forward.

Over the next few years, Bohr became increasingly vocal about the Nazis' cruel and rapidly intensifying anti-Semitic policies. When the theoretical physicist was summoned to speak at the International Congress of Anthropological and Ethnological Sciences, he concluded his speech with a call to action. As Denmark publicly and vigorously branded itself a "neutral" state, Bohr knew that he could not vilify Hitler by name. Instead, he reminded the audience to rise above discrimination and all forms of hatred in the name of science, and he underscored the importance and priceless value of multicultural cooperation.

During this period, Bohr continued his collaboration with Meitner, as well as her now relocated nephew. The physicist had already founded the "Liquid Drop Model" of the nucleus, which theorized that the nucleus would remain intact, but to his great surprise, Frisch and Meitner unearthed a method to stretch a single drop into two. To do so, they were essentially substituting resistant forces with the electric charges of the nucleus, a split that would result in the discharge of 200,000,000 electron volts. Frisch recalled how a flustered and somewhat crimson-cheeked Bohr slapped his forehead at the revelation. Still, he gave Frisch a hearty pat on the back and encouraged him to complete his paper on the splitting of the nucleus, a process they later named "fission." It was apparently Bohr, one of Frisch's primary mentors, who identified uranium, with its atomic weight of 235, as an isotope that was more susceptible to fission.

One of the most imposing obstacles the researchers faced was the unbalanced equation, since the energy it took to split the atom was far greater than the charge produced after the division. In time, Bohr and his peers were able to prove that a greater charge could be manufactured by creating a "chain reaction," set off by the neutrons discharged during the process of fission. Enrico Fermi, the naturalized American physicist who spearheaded the research, published his results in March 1939. That same day, he convened with the Chief of Naval Operations and outlined to him the enticing prospect of utilizing his findings in an "explosive of unimaginable power."

Fermi

As Fermi negotiated, his partner, Leo Szilard, called for an urgent conference with Bohr and numerous other physicists to discuss the potential repercussions of their findings. Although some, such as Bohr, voiced their misgivings about contributing to such an instrument of destruction, the group eventually decided to resume their research, if only because they feared that the Germans would soon overtake them on the same path. Bohr was further disturbed by the secrecy such a project entailed, for complete transparency was a policy he usually favored. However, understanding that secrecy would serve a greater good, he put such thoughts to rest.

Szilard

Around the time World War II started, Bohr was temporarily boarding at Princeton's Institute for Advanced Study. Due to the worsening situation in Denmark, his foreign colleagues advised him to send for his family and remain in New Jersey, but the patriotic physicist could not bear to part with his nation and beloved institute. Not long after his return to Denmark, in April 1940, the Germans invaded, bringing about the Danes' inevitable surrender. The U.S. Embassy offered him a ticket to America, but Bohr, thinking of his Jewish mother and relatives, chose to stay put. He explained, "I [felt] it to be my duty in our desperate situation to help resist the threat against the freedom of our institutions and to assist in the protection of the exiled scientists who have sought refuge here."

The offers did not stop there, but Bohr refused to consider them until he was informed about an outstanding warrant for his arrest in 1943. Days later, the Bohr family swiftly packed up their belongings, smuggled themselves onto an obscure fishing vessel, and headed for Sweden.

Bohr's spirit remained unbroken, even as he had become a refugee. In the weeks leading up to the mass arrests of Jews in Denmark, he worked overseas to provide funding and resources for the resistance of his home country. In the end, he personally aided in the relocation and ultimate salvation of nearly 6,000 Jews, all of whom were to be provisionally housed in Sweden.

Later in 1943, Bohr traveled to London, where he had been summoned by the heads of an ultra-classified program established by the British and Canadian governments. The collaboration, captained by James Chadwick, was involved in the development of various nuclear weapons, nicknamed "tube alloys." In 1944, Bohr was summoned to the United States once again to participate in the Manhattan Project, a covert operation aiming to establish nuclear bombs packed with plutonium and uranium. – a formidable part of their plan to topple the Axis powers. Bohr and his son Aage, who accompanied him and worked alongside him during his tenure at the Los Alamos National Laboratory in New Mexico, received code names of their own. Niels became Nicholas Baker, and his son was James Baker.

Aage Bohr

An excerpt from Bohr's progress report to British Prime Minister Winston Churchill in 1944 noted, "What until a few years ago might be considered as a fantastic dream is at present being realized within great laboratories and huge production plants secretly erected in some of the most solitary regions of the United States. There a larger group of physicists than ever before collected for a single purpose, working hand in hand with a whole army of engineers and technicians...preparing new materials capable of an immense energy release...One cannot help comparing the situation with that of the alchemists of former days, groping in the dark in their vain efforts to make gold..."

Meanwhile, Bohr launched a campaign for nuclear awareness on the side. He met regularly with British and American leaders and urged them to inform the Soviet Union about the true depths of their nuclear projects before the war's end. He promoted, as his principles dictated, all-encompassing transparency, which he believed would reinforce peaceful global relations altogether.

When Japan chose to ignore the ultimatum given by the Allies at the Potsdam Conference, President Harry Truman chose to use the atomic bombs developed by the Manhattan Project. Truman took the scientists' concerns into account, but the deadly experience of Okinawa made clear that hundreds of thousands of Americans would be casualties in a conventional invasion of the mainland of Japan. Moreover, the fanatical manner in which Japanese soldiers and civilians held out on Okinawa indicated that the Japanese would suffer more casualties during an invasion than they would if the bombs were used. Pursuant to the Quebec Agreement, Canada and Great Britain consented to the use of the bomb. As a result, Truman authorized its use on two sites in Japan.

Once Truman gave the go ahead to use the bomb, there was still a matter of picking out sites. Though largely forgotten today, the U.S. listed sites in Japan that had the most military value when choosing where to hit. Moreover, the Americans had to deal with weather conditions, which doomed Nagasaki on August 9.

With the bombings of Hiroshima and Nagasaki marking the end of World War II, the Manhattan Project went from top secret to public knowledge. Just a year after the war's end, Congress began debating what to do with its new nuclear arsenal and how to control the deadly technology. Out of this came the Atomic Energy Act of 1946, proposed by Senator Brien McMahon of Connecticut. It passed the Senate unanimously and also passed overwhelmingly in the House. It was signed by President Truman on August 1, 1946, going into effect on January 1, 1947. The Atomic Energy Act created the United States Atomic Energy Commission to ensure that future developments in nuclear technology were overseen by Congress. The law also restricted the ability of the United States to share nuclear knowledge with other nations, a proviso that offended Great Britain and Canada, who had contributed to the Manhattan Project and had shared information with the U.S. during the war. As a result of the Atomic Energy Act, both nations were forced to decide whether or not to pursue their own separate nuclear energy programs.

Another lasting issue that came out of the Manhattan Project was the global nuclear arms race it ignited. As some scientists warned, the bombings of Hiroshima and Nagasaki ignited an arms race between the Soviet Union and the United States. Arms races sprung up elsewhere in the world, notably between India and Pakistan, and nations around the world have continued to pursue nuclear weapons. The attacks on Japan solidified the idea that ownership of nuclear technology permanently insulated a nation from external attack, as no nation would threaten to attack such a power out of fear of nuclear retaliation.

For his part, Bohr continued his campaign for nuclear transparency well after he returned to Denmark in 1945. Five years later, he took the podium once again and recited his open letter to the United Nations regarding his stance on "international cooperation on nuclear energy." He said, "Humanity will be confronted with dangers of unprecedented character unless, in due time, measures can be taken to forestall a disastrous competition in such formidable armaments and to establish an international control of the manufacture and use of powerful materials."

In 1955, a decade after his return to Denmark, Bohr and his colleagues worked to build the Risø experimental research facility, and they installed in it a modern accelerator designed for the purpose of researching the safe and peaceful use of nuclear energy. He was also one of the original founders of the European Center for Nuclear Research, serving as the head of the institute's theoretical department for five years. In 1957, Bohr's endeavors towards international nuclear relations were recognized when he was presented with the first-ever medal for Atoms for Peace.

In the autumn of 1962, Niels suffered a stroke that left him bedridden, and at the age of 77, his frail heart finally gave out on November 18 of that year. His body was cremated, and his encased ashes laid to rest in the Bohr section of the Assistens Cemetery in Copenhagen. Three years after his death, the Copenhagen Institute of Theoretical Physics was rebranded as the Niels Bohr Institute. Today, the thriving institute consists of a set of 10 buildings laid out between Blegdamsvej and Faelledparken, and equipped with over 1,000 students and staff members who have now branched into not just quantum physics, but geophysics, particle physics, astronomy, biophysics, and nanophysics.

The Niels Bohr Institute

In 1975, Aage Bohr received the Nobel Prize "for the discovery of the connection between collective motion and particle motion in atomic nuclei and the development of the theory of the structure of the atomic nucleus based on this connection." This made Niels and Aage one of only six pairs of father-son Nobel laureates. Six years later, a band of German researchers produced a new atom through a mixture of bismuth and chromium atoms, one that is now called "Bohrium."

Bohr's influence remains palpable to this very day. Not only is his word still considered canon by many modern scientists, he is commemorated through dozens of plaques, busts, statues, and other monuments. His face was even featured on the now-retired Danish 500 Kroner, and his famous model is depicted in the logo of the U.S. Atomic Energy Commission. It is difficult to find words that would encapsulate the brilliance and legacy of Niels Bohr, but his former colleague, Georg von Hevesy, may have done him justice when he said, "Centuries may elapse until a man like him will be born again."

Online Resources

Other books about scientists by Charles River Editors

Other books about Bohr on Amazon

Further Reading

Waldek, S. *13 Facts About Physicist Niels Bohr*. 9 July 2018, mentalfloss.com/article/544594/facts-about-physicist-niels-bohr. Accessed 8 Oct. 2018.

Editors, L N. *NIELS BOHR | 10 FACTS ON THE FAMOUS DANISH SCIENTIST*. 1 June 2016, learnodo-newtonic.com/niels-bohr-facts. Accessed 9 Oct. 2018.

Editors, S S. *Niels Bohr Facts*. 2018, www.softschools.com/facts/scientists/niels_bohr_facts/724/. Accessed 9 Oct. 2018.

Editors, N 18. *Niels Bohr's 127th Birthday: Top 10 Interesting Facts*. 7 Oct. 2012, www.news18.com/news/india/niels-bohrs-127th-birthday-top-10-interesting-facts-514991.html. Accessed 9 Oct. 2018.

Editors, T F. *30 Fun And Interesting Facts About Niels Bohr*. 23 June 2018, tonsoffacts.com/30-fun-and-interesting-facts-about-niels-bohr/. Accessed 9 Oct. 2018.

Editors, N P. *Niels Henrik David Bohr - Biographical*. 2017, www.nobelprize.org/prizes/physics/1922/bohr/biographical/. Accessed 9 Oct. 2018.

Editors, M. *Niels Bohr: 10 Things You Need to Know about the Physicist and Nobel Prize Winner*. 7 Oct. 2012, www.mirror.co.uk/news/uk-news/niels-bohr-10-things-you-1365579. Accessed 9 Oct. 2018.

Editors, F S. *Niels Bohr*. 19 Dec. 2015, www.famousscientists.org/niels-bohr/. Accessed 9 Oct. 2018.

Editors, I F. *10 Interesting Niels Bohr Facts*. 28 Aug. 2014, www.myinterestingfacts.com/niels-bohr-facts/. Accessed 9 Oct. 2018.

Editors, Y D. *Niels Henrik David Bohr Facts*. 2010, biography.yourdictionary.com/niels-henrik-david-bohr. Accessed 9 Oct. 2018.

Editors, B. *Niels Bohr Biography*. 2 Apr. 2014, www.biography.com/people/niels-bohr-21010897. Accessed 9 Oct. 2018.

Aaserud, F. *Niels Bohr*. 3 Oct. 2018, www.britannica.com/biography/Niels-Bohr. Accessed 9 Oct. 2018.

Palermo, E. *Niels Bohr: Biography & Atomic Theory*. 28 Aug. 2017, www.livescience.com/32016-niels-bohr-atomic-theory.html. Accessed 9 Oct. 2018.

Obi, J. *Niels Bohr Timeline*. 28 Sept. 2012, prezi.com/8k7zg2_aojw2/niels-bohr-timeline/. Accessed 9 Oct. 2018.

Editors, F P. *Niels Bohr Biography*. 15 Sept. 2017, www.thefamouspeople.com/profiles/niels-henrik-david-bohr-2446.php. Accessed 9 Oct. 2018.

Editors, T T. *Neils Bohr's Life*. 2017, www.timetoast.com/timelines/neils-bohrs-life. Accessed 9 Oct. 2018.

Editors, M E. *Niels Henrik David Bohr (1885-1962)*. 13 Nov. 2015, micro.magnet.fsu.edu/optics/timeline/people/bohr.html. Accessed 9 Oct. 2018.

Juncher, D. *Niels Bohr's Childhood*. 2017, www.nbi.ku.dk/english/www/niels/bohr/barndom/. Accessed 10 Oct. 2018.

Juncher, D. *Niels Bohr's School Years*. 2017, www.nbi.ku.dk/english/www/niels/bohr/skole/. Accessed 10 Oct. 2018.

Juncher, D. *Life as a Student*. 2017, www.nbi.ku.dk/english/www/niels/bohr/universitetet/. Accessed 10 Oct. 2018.

Editors, U S. *Niels Henrik David Bohr (1885-1962)*. Oct. 2003, www-groups.dcs.st-and.ac.uk/history/Biographies/Bohr_Niels.html. Accessed 10 Oct. 2018.

Crutcher, T. *Niels Henrik David Bohr*. 2011, physics.eou.edu/students/crutcher/Bohr. Accessed 10 Oct. 2018.

Editors, E C. *Bohr, Niels Henrik David*. 2008, www.encyclopedia.com/people/science-and-technology/physics-biographies/niels-henrik-david-bohr. Accessed 10 Oct. 2018.

Editors, M H. *Niels Bohr*. 22 Feb. 2013, myhero.com/N_Bohr_mva_US_2013. Accessed 10 Oct. 2018.

Good, G. *The Bohrs: Physics Runs in the Family*. 27 Jan. 2014, www.aip.org/commentary/bohrs-physics-runs-family. Accessed 10 Oct. 2018.

Editors, H B. *Niels Bohr*. 5 May 2004, www.histclo.com/bio/b/bio-bohrn.html. Accessed 10 Oct. 2018.

Chestnutt, B. *Niels Bohr: Biography, Atomic Theory & Discovery*. 2016, study.com/academy/lesson/niels-bohr-biography-atomic-theory-discovery.html. Accessed 10 Oct. 2018.

Mukunda, N. *The Life and Work of Niels Bohr – A Brief Sketch*. Oct. 2013, www.ias.ac.in/article/fulltext/reso/018/10/0877-0884. Accessed 10 Oct. 2018.

Favrholdt, D. *Niels Bohr's Philosophical Background*. 1992, www.royalacademy.dk/Publications/Low/709_Favrholdt, David.pdf. Accessed 10 Oct. 2018.

Editors, I P. *Neil Bohr's Life*. 2009, ishiaampeloquio.weebly.com/. Accessed 10 Oct. 2018.

Jones, A Z. *Niels Bohr - Biographical Profile*. 18 Mar. 2017, www.thoughtco.com/niels-bohr-biographical-profile-2699055. Accessed 10 Oct. 2018.

Editors, C M. *Niels Bohr*. 2017, www.cs.mcgill.ca/~rwest/wikispeedia/wpcd/wp/n/Niels_Bohr.htm. Accessed 10 Oct. 2018.

O'Connor, J J, and E F Robertson. *Niels Bohr (1885 - 1962)*. 2015, www.jewishvirtuallibrary.org/niels-bohr. Accessed 10 Oct. 2018.

Editors, T H. *Niels Bohr*. 2012, totallyhistory.com/niels-bohr/. Accessed 10 Oct. 2018.

Rhodes, R. *The Philosopher Physicist*. 26 Jan. 1992, www.nytimes.com/1992/01/26/books/the-philosopher-physicist.html. Accessed 10 Oct. 2018.

Butterworth, J. *Niels Bohr: Life Behind the Physics*. 3 June 2015, www.theguardian.com/science/life-and-physics/2015/jun/03/niels-bohr-life-behind-the-physics. Accessed 11 Oct. 2018.

Cessna, A. *Niels Bohr*. 25 Jan. 2010, www.universetoday.com/52069/niels-bohr/. Accessed 11 Oct. 2018.

Editors, S N. *NIELS BOHR SUMMARY*. 2018, www.sparknotes.com/biography/bohr/summary/. Accessed 11 Oct. 2018.

Ramsey, S C. *The Early Years*. 2011, msu.edu/~ramseys3/lbs171h/index.htm. Accessed 11 Oct. 2018.

Ramsey, S C. *The Innovations Begin*. 2011, msu.edu/~ramseys3/lbs171h/index_files/Page349.htm. Accessed 11 Oct. 2018.

Editors, P U. *NIELS BOHR (1885 - 1962)*. 2014, www.physicsoftheuniverse.com/scientists_bohr.html. Accessed 11 Oct. 2018.

Simkin, J. *Niels Bohr*. Aug. 2014, spartacus-educational.com/USAbohr.htm. Accessed 11 Oct. 2018.

Crepeau, B. *Niels Bohr*. 1 Jan. 2006,
www.georgiastandards.org/resources/Lexile_in_Action/SPS1_1170.pdf. Accessed 11 Oct. 2018.

Editors, H V. *Niels Bohr*. 2015, hollowverse.com/niels-bohr/. Accessed 11 Oct. 2018.

Popova, M. *Nobel-Winning Physicist Niels Bohr on Subjective vs. Objective Reality and the Uses of Religion in a Secular World*. 1 Feb. 2018, www.brainpickings.org/2018/02/01/niels-bohr-science-religion/. Accessed 11 Oct. 2018.

Helm, M. *Bohr's Model of the Atom Explains Science in Everyday Life*. 20 Sept. 2018, scitech.au.dk/en/roemer/apr13/bohrs-model-of-the-atom-explains-science-in-everyday-life/. Accessed 11 Oct. 2018.

Editors, S C. *Electrons - Real-Life Applications*. 18 May 2001, www.scienceclarified.com/everyday/Real-Life-Chemistry-Vol-1/Electrons-Real-life-applications.html. Accessed 11 Oct. 2018.

Oullette, J. *Don't Be Dissin' the Bohr Model!* 9 Feb. 2012, blogs.scientificamerican.com/cocktail-party-physics/dont-be-dissin-the-bohr-model/. Accessed 11 Oct. 2018.

Csanady, A. *Meet the Man Who Gave Us Atomic Theory and the Bomb: Niels Bohr's Grandson in Conversation*. 3 June 2015, nationalpost.com/news/world/meet-the-man-who-gave-us-atomic-theory-and-the-bomb-niels-bohrs-grandson-in-conversation. Accessed 11 Oct. 2018.

Editors, T C. *Why Denmark Dominates the World Happiness Report Rankings Year after Year*. 20 Mar. 2018, theconversation.com/why-denmark-dominates-the-world-happiness-report-rankings-year-after-year-93542. Accessed 11 Oct. 2018.

Colson, T. *7 Reasons Denmark Is the Happiest Country in the World*. 26 Sept. 2016, www.independent.co.uk/news/world/europe/7-reasons-denmark-is-the-happiest-country-in-the-world-a7331146.html. Accessed 11 Oct. 2018.

Long, D. *THE ATOMIC BOMB AND BEYOND*. 2006, www.doug-long.com/bohr.htm. Accessed 11 Oct. 2018.

Editors, W C. *Mechanism vs. Vitalism*. 2012, wildernesschiropractic.com/mechanism-vs-vitalism/. Accessed 11 Oct. 2018.

Allen, G E. *Mechanism, Vitalism and Organicism in Late Nineteenth and Twentieth-Century Biology: the Importance of Historical Context*. Mar. 2005, www.sciencedirect.com/science/article/pii/S1369848605000191. Accessed 11 Oct. 2018.

Editors, G. *Professor Christian Harald Lauritz Peter Emil Bohr, Dr. Med.* 22 July 2017, www.geni.com/people/Christian-Bohr/6000000002437569232. Accessed 11 Oct. 2018.

Gignac, S. *Love, Literature, and the Quantum Atom.* 2017, www.aip.org/history-programs/news/love-literature-and-quantum-atom. Accessed 11 Oct. 2018.

Editors, R. *Danish Folkeskole Education.* 30 July 2016, www.revolvy.com/page/Danish-Folkeskole-Education. Accessed 11 Oct. 2018.

Juncher, D. *Bohr's Atomic Model.* 2017, www.nbi.ku.dk/english/www/niels/bohr/bohratomet/. Accessed 11 Oct. 2018.

Palmer, J. *Niels Bohr Letters Reveal Trials of His Time in England.* 17 Apr. 2013, www.bbc.com/news/science-environment-22174013. Accessed 11 Oct. 2018.

Cassidy, D. *Student Years: University Student.* 2015, history.aip.org/exhibits/heisenberg/p05.htm. Accessed 12 Oct. 2018.

Editors, P S. *Bohr's Tall Story.* 2017, felix.physics.sunysb.edu/~allen/Jokes/bohr.html. Accessed 12 Oct. 2018.

Heilbron, J L. *J. J. Thomson and the Bohr Atom.* 1 Apr. 1977, physicstoday.scitation.org/doi/10.1063/1.3037496. Accessed 12 Oct. 2018.

Editors, S N. *To Manchester with Rutherford.* 2017, www.sparknotes.com/biography/bohr/section3/. Accessed 12 Oct. 2018.

Editors, U P. *Niels Bohr.* 2012, chemed.chem.purdue.edu/genchem/history/bohr.html. Accessed 12 Oct. 2018.

Editors, M R. *Determination of the Surface-Tension of Water by the Method of Jet Vibration.* 2017, www.manhattanrarebooks.com/pages/books/309/niels-bohr/determination-of-the-surface-tension-of-water-by-the-method-of-jet-vibration. Accessed 12 Oct. 2018.

Editors, K U. *Unruly Plasmas: Researchers Challenge Bohr-Van Leeuwen Theorem.* 7 Aug. 2013, phys.org/news/2013-08-unruly-plasmas-bohr-van-leeuwen-theorem.html. Accessed 12 Oct. 2018.

Editors, S N. *War and Manchester.* 2017, www.sparknotes.com/biography/bohr/section4/. Accessed 12 Oct. 2018.

Ball, P. *The Making of Niels Bohr.* 7 Aug. 2013, www.newscientist.com/article/mg21929291-100-the-making-of-niels-bohr/. Accessed 12 Oct. 2018.

Ramsey, S C. *Bohr's Model of the Hydrogen Atom*. 2017, msu.edu/~ramseys3/lbs171h/index_files/Page419.htm. Accessed 12 Oct. 2018.

Juncher, D. *Niels Bohr Institute*. 2017, www.nbi.ku.dk/english/www/niels/bohr/institutet/. Accessed 12 Oct. 2018.

Juncher, D. *The Nobel Prize*. 2017, www.nbi.ku.dk/english/www/niels/bohr/nobelprisen/. Accessed 12 Oct. 2018.

Juncher, D. *Nuclear Physics and War*. 2017, www.nbi.ku.dk/english/www/niels/bohr/kernefysik/. Accessed 12 Oct. 2018.

Editors, N P. *Joseph John Thomson*. 2018, www.nobelprize.org/prizes/physics/1906/thomson/biographical/. Accessed 12 Oct. 2018.

Editors, R. *Ernest Rutherford*. 25 Sept. 2018, www.revolvy.com/page/Ernest-Rutherford. Accessed 12 Oct. 2018.

Editors, N P. *The Nobel Prize in Physics 1922*. 2017, www.nobelprize.org/prizes/physics/1922/summary/. Accessed 12 Oct. 2018.

Knapp, A. *For Winning The Nobel Prize, Niels Bohr Got A House With Free Beer*. 28 Nov. 2012, www.forbes.com/sites/alexknapp/2012/11/28/for-winning-the-nobel-prize-niels-bohr-got-a-house-with-free-beer/#50b231727595. Accessed 12 Oct. 2018.

Juncher, D. *The Carlsberg Honorary Residence* . 2017, www.nbi.ku.dk/english/www/historical_sites/physical_science/the_carlsberg_honorary_residenc e/. Accessed 12 Oct. 2018.

Editors, S N. *War and Personal Tragedy*. 2018, www.sparknotes.com/biography/bohr/section7/. Accessed 12 Oct. 2018.

Editors, S N. *Splitting the Atom*. 2018, www.sparknotes.com/biography/bohr/section8/. Accessed 12 Oct. 2018.

Editors, S N. *The Bomb*. 2018, www.sparknotes.com/biography/bohr/section9/. Accessed 12 Oct. 2018.

Juncher, D. *The Final Years*. 2017, www.nbi.ku.dk/english/www/niels/bohr/de_sidste_aar/. Accessed 12 Oct. 2018.

Nielsen, J. R. (1972). *Early Work (1905 - 1911)* (Vol. 1, Niels Bohr - Collected Works (Book 1)). North Holland.

Spangenburg, R., & Moser, D. K. (2009). *Niels Bohr, Revised Edition*. Infobase Publishing.

Free Books by Charles River Editors

We have brand new titles available for free most days of the week. To see which of our titles are currently free, click on this link.

Discounted Books by Charles River Editors

We have titles at a discount price of just 99 cents everyday. To see which of our titles are currently 99 cents, <u>click on this link</u>.

Made in the USA
Columbia, SC
17 December 2019